D1629806
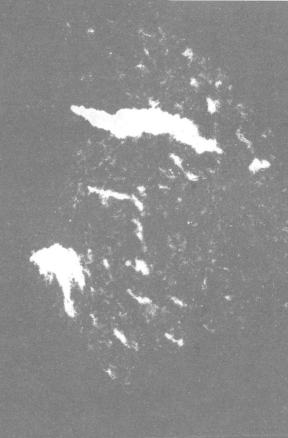

Up the Garden Path

Are you a Ladybird?

KINGFISHER
Kingfisher Publications Plc
New Penderel House
283-288 High Holborn
London WC1V 7HZ

First published by Kingfisher Publications Plc 2000

2 4 6 8 10 9 7 5 3 1 (hb)

2(BCA)0600/TWP/DIG/150NYMA

2 4 6 8 10 9 7 5 3 1 (pb)

1SBF/1RH/0500/TWP/DIG(DIG)/150NYMA

A CIP catalogue record for this book is available from
the British Library.

ISBN 0 7534 0420 6 (hb)
ISBN 0 7534 0530 X (pb)

Editor: Katie Puckett
Series Designer: Jane Tassie

Printed in Singapore

Are you a Ladybird?

Judy Allen and Tudor Humphries

KING*fisher*

Are you a ladybird?

If you are,
your parents look like this,
and they eat aphids.

When your
mother lays
her eggs, you are
inside one of them.

While you're
in there,
grOW.

When you have grown big enough,
break out of the egg.

You have a lot of brothers and sisters. If you look at them you may think you have all made a big mistake.

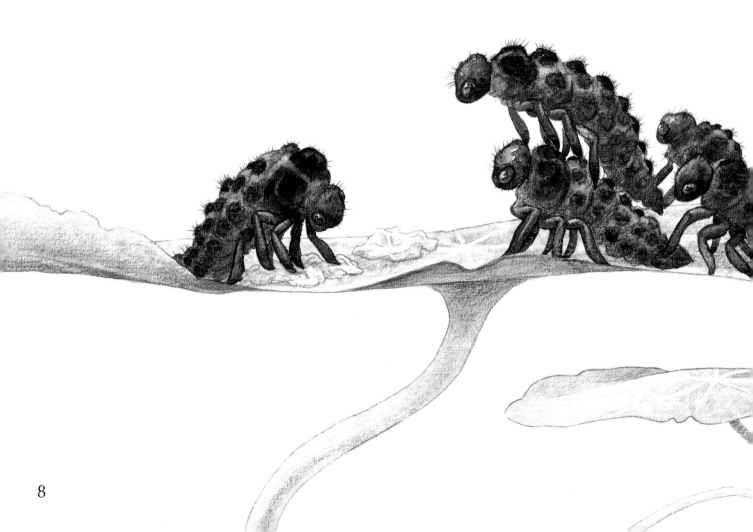

Not one of you is the same shape as
a ladybird. Not one of you is the same
colour as a ladybird.

Don't worry about this. Just eat.

Eat your own eggshell first.

Then eat aphids.

Eat lots of aphids.

They are easy to catch
and they are very nourishing.

As you grow bigger,
your skin will feel tight.

This is not a problem.

Soon, it will split down the middle.

Wriggle out of it

and take it off.

Then eat more aphids.

As you grow, you must take your skin off again – and again. Each time there is a new one underneath.

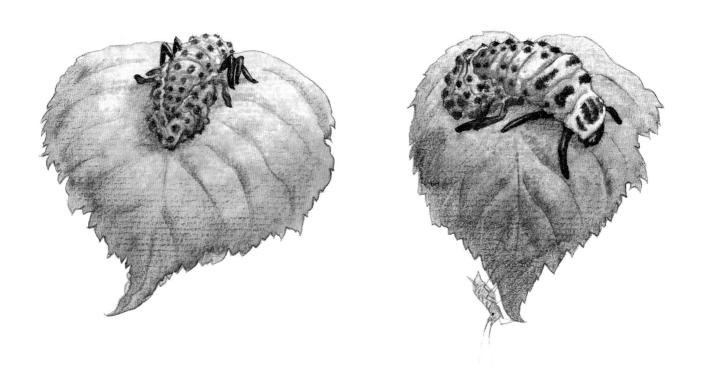

Keep eating the aphids.

One day you will feel very tired.
Stop eating. Curl up like this.

Take off your skin one more time.
Now, wait for your new skin to grow hard.

When your hard skin splits,
climb out of it one last time.

Now you are the right shape,
but you are not the right colour.
You are very, very pale.

Just wait...

17

Slowly,
slowly,
slowly,
your colour
grows stronger.

Your black dots appear.

18

Congratulations,
you're a
ladybird!

You can fly!

You are very hungry,
so you had better look for
something to eat.

Aphids will do nicely.

23

However,
if your parents
look a bit like this

or this

or this

you are not a ladybird.

You are...

... a human child.

Your skin will not split as you grow.

You can't fly.

Also, it is very unlikely that you are red with black dots.

Never mind, you can do a great
many things that ladybirds can't do.

And you will never, ever,
EVER have to eat aphids.

Did You Know...

...a female ladybird
can eat about 70
aphids a day, but
the smaller male ladybird
only eats about 40 a day.

...there are more than 5000 different kinds of ladybird. They are not all red with black spots – some are black with red spots...

...or yellow with black spots, or red with yellow-and-black spots...

...these are 7-spot ladybirds, but you might see a 2-spot or a 5-spot or even a yellow-and-black 22-spot.

...ladybirds are not dangerous to humans – but they can bite.

...animals and birds won't eat ladybirds because they taste horrible.